DEEPER

A Christian Mother – Daughter Journal

ANDREA GARDINER

I dedicate this journal to Zoe, who designed
the cover for me. A wonderful mother, a
precious cousin: you and your three little ones
are sorely missed. Shine brightly with the
angels xx

Contents

Acknowledgements

I would like to thank Zoe for her artwork, inspiration and hard work with me on this project.

I would also like to thank my first readers for their encouragement and ideas.

Thanks too to the girls in the Project Ecuador club, who trialled many of the activities included in this journal. It is such fun leading you to a deeper relationship with our Lord and your families.

Thank you to my husband for his encouragement and suggestions, and most of all to my three wonderful daughters who are such a blessing to us both.

Introduction

Welcome to this journey of discovery, this opportunity to share what is really on your mind and heart. This journal can be a special way of communicating in the midst of our hectic, modern lives. As you record your thought and feelings, you will also be creating a unique chronicle to treasure and cherish in the years to come.

The mother-daughter relationship is a very special one. The bond of love between you is very strong. During the teenage years, daughters are discovering who they are, becoming independent, learning to fend for themselves and stretching their wings. Sometimes this natural stage of life can lead to friction, as mothers still want to care for and protect their daughters, while daughters can feel that they are being over-protective or restrictive. Good communication is vital to enable misunderstandings to be cleared up and for that bond of love to deepen and to grow.

So what is the purpose of writing in a journal together? There are many potential benefits. The fun list, drawing prompts, open questions and Scripture reflections will enable you to get to know things about each other you never thought to ask. They will open up important topics of conversation and will allow you to think through many common issues facing girls and women today. They will prompt you to reflect on your faith, and how it helps you on a daily basis. You will be creating a record that you will enjoy looking back on in the years to come.

When my daughter was learning to write, and even though she did not enjoy writing, she started jotting down notes and passing them to me whenever she was upset. She knew that they would grab my attention. She also knew that she would receive a much more measured response than she would have, had she come weeping and wailing. When we have strong emotions about something, it can help to write about it. Putting pen to paper can help defuse the situation and invites a considered response. It also means those important thoughts, questions and memories are not forgotten in life's busyness. There are plenty of blank pages included in the journal, so that you can jot down what's on your mind. As you make a note of that problem you encountered or funny event in your day, you are ensuring that it is shared and addressed.

We find it embarrassing to talk about some subjects. Writing down the questions that you are uncomfortable mentioning can be a very useful way of making sure that you discuss them. As you pass your journal back and forth between you, you will develop the confidence to write about any subject and find your relationship deepens.

The journal is there to help you have the conversations that are important to you. You do not have to complete it in order or indeed fill in every detail. Find the topics that are most relevant and interesting to you at that moment. Use the blank pages to write or ask about anything at all that is on your mind. Take your time over filling in your journal. There is no rush. Put a bookmark in it to show the other person where you have been writing, so that they can read it and respond. Don't forget to let the other person know when you have written something, so that you receive a timely reply!

One last piece of advice – do make sure that this journal is confidential between the two of you. You need to know that what you write is for your eyes only, or you will not write what is truly on your heart.

Enjoy the fun, share your joys, worries and questions, and never forget that the most important thing is your love for each other.

All about us

Daughter

My Favourite ...

- Film _____
- Song _____
- Bible character _____
- Book _____
- Sport _____
- Place _____
- Memory _____
- Food _____
- Colour _____
- Recipe _____
- Animal _____
- Month _____
- Part of the body _____
- Subject _____
- Craft _____
- Musical instrument _____
- Ice-cream flavour _____
- Chocolate bar _____
- Verse in the Bible _____
- Game _____

Mother

My Favourite...

- Film _____
- Song _____
- Bible character _____
- Book _____
- Sport _____
- Place _____
- Memory _____
- Food _____
- Colour _____
- Recipe _____
- Animal _____
- Month _____
- Part of the body _____
- Subject _____
- Craft _____
- Musical instrument _____
- Ice-cream flavour _____
- Chocolate bar _____
- Verse in the Bible _____
- Game _____

Fill this with your own thoughts...

Daughter

Write a letter to your mum telling her why you love her, what you most appreciate about her, the best thing she has ever done for you and a favourite memory of something you did together.

Love You♡

Dear Mum,

_____

_____

_____

_____

_____

_____

_____

_____

_____

_____

_____

_____

_____

_____

_____

_____

love from

Mother

Write a letter to your daughter telling her why you love her, what you most appreciate about her, the best thing she has ever done for you and a favourite memory of something you did together.

Dear _____ ,

_____

_____

_____

_____

_____

_____

_____

_____

_____

_____

_____

_____

_____

_____

_____

Love from

Daughter

Annotate and draw on this outline to show what kind of person you are, what you like to do, and what is important to you. For example if you like baking you might draw some cookies in your hands, if you are kind you could draw yourself with a large heart, and if the Bible is important to you, you could draw a Bible by your head. Try to make your drawing express who you are.

Mother

Annotate and draw on this outline to show what kind of person you are, what you like to do, and what is important to you. For example if you like baking you might draw some cookies in your hands, if you are kind you could draw yourself with a large heart, and if the Bible is important to you, you could draw a Bible by your head. Try to make your drawing express who you are.

Fill this with your own thoughts...

_____
_____
_____
_____
_____
_____
_____
_____
_____
_____
_____
_____
_____
_____
_____
_____
_____
_____
_____
_____
_____
_____
_____
_____
_____

Daughter

Write a prayer for your mum. You might like to include words of thanks for her, to ask for help for her for problems she is facing, and to ask God to bless her in certain areas of her life. Is there anything you need to say sorry for in relation to your mum? Have you treated her badly at all recently? Is there anything your mum needs right now that you want to ask God for?

Our Father in heaven,

_____

_____

_____

_____

_____

_____

_____

_____

_____

_____

_____

_____

_____

_____

_____

_____

in Jesus name, Amen.

Mother

Write a prayer for your daughter. You might like to include words of thanks for her, to ask for help for her for problems she is facing, and to ask God to bless her in certain areas of her life. Is there anything you need to say sorry for in relation to your daughter? Have you treated her badly at all recently? Is there anything your daughter needs right now that you want to ask God for?

Our Father in heaven,

_____

_____

_____

_____

_____

_____

_____

_____

_____

_____

_____

_____

_____

_____

_____

In Jesus name, Amen

Fill this with your own thoughts...

Mother & Daughter

What do you think God is saying to you about your relationship?

_____

_____

_____

_____

_____

_____

_____

_____

_____

_____

_____

_____

_____

_____

_____

_____

_____

_____

_____

_____

_____

_____

_____

_____

All about you

Mother

How did you feel when you found out you were expecting me (your daughter)? _____

_____

_____

Tell me about my birth. How was I born, and where? How did you feel?

_____

_____

_____

What was I like when I was a baby?

_____

_____

_____

How old was I when I cut my first tooth, took my first step and said my first words? _____

_____

_____

What were my first words? _____

_____

_____

Which foods did I like to eat when I was a toddler? _____

_____

What were my favourite nursery rhymes and stories?

_____

_____

_____

23

Daughter

What is your earliest memory?

_____

_____

_____

Do you remember anything that scared you when you were younger?

_____

_____

_____

What is your happiest memory from when you were little?

_____

_____

_____

Do you remember a time when you were sad when you were younger?

_____

_____

_____

Do you remember your first tooth coming out? What happened?

_____

_____

Do you have any questions for your mum about when you were little?

_____

_____

_____

_____

Continue your conversation here ...

"For you created my inmost being; you knit me together in my mother's womb. I praise you because I am fearfully and wonderfully made; your works are wonderful, I know that full well. My frame was not hidden from you when I was made in the secret place. When I was woven together in the depths of the earth, your eyes saw my unformed body. All the days ordained for me were written in your book before one of them came to be." Psalm 139:13-16

Daughter:

How are you described in these verses? _____
_____
_____

How does that make you feel? _____
_____
_____

Sometimes mums describe their baby as an "accident" or a "surprise". How does God see each new baby that is born? _____
_____

"I have loved you with an everlasting love." Jeremiah 31:3

Mother:

God speaks these words over your daughter. How does that make you feel? _____
_____

Write some words of advice to your daughter to read whenever she feels lonely, sad, inadequate or let down. Let her know how precious she is to you, and to her Heavenly Father. _____
_____
_____
_____
_____

Continue your conversation here ...

27

Daughter

Think of the times when you feel most happy and fulfilled. What are you doing? What talents, hobbies or passions do you have that make you feel most alive? _____

_____

_____

How much time each week do you spend doing these hobbies or activities? Who does them with you? _____

_____

_____

Who supports you in these pursuits? Do you have the support you need to be able to develop these talents and interests? _____

_____

_____

Is there anything your mum could do to help you develop these interests further? _____

_____

_____

_____

Do you know what your mum's passions and hobbies are? List them here.

_____

_____

_____

_____

_____

_____

Mother

What were your favourite hobbies or interests when you were the age your daughter is now? _____

_____

Do you still have the same interests and passions or have they changed over the years? _____

_____

_____

Did anyone support you in developing your hobbies and talents when you were young? Do you have time to pursue them now? _____

_____

_____

What are your daughter´s hobbies and passions? When is she happiest?

_____

_____

_____

What support does she have/need to pursue her interests?

_____

_____

_____

Is there anything you would like to tell her about her talents?

_____

_____

_____

_____

Quick Beauty Quiz
Answer true or false

	Mother	Daughter
1. You must wash your hair every day.		
2. It is necessary to shave or wax your legs.		
3. The minimum SPF sunblock you should use to protect your skin from the sun's rays is SPF 15.		
4. While you are menstruating, it is particularly important to wash frequently.		
5. Your doctor can help treat your acne if over the counter products are not working.		
6. Smoking helps you look beautiful.		
7. Getting plenty of sleep, drinking water, eating healthily and moisturizing all help you have beautiful skin.		
8. The main purpose of exercise is to make you look toned and beautiful.		
9. If you are overweight, it is impossible to look beautiful.		
10. You must wear make-up if you want to look beautiful.		

Answers: 1 F, 2 F, 3 T (higher if possible), 4 T (your skin becomes greasy and body odour increases), 5 T (there are many options available), 6 F (smoking damages your skin), 7 T, 8 F (exercise is important to have a healthy body), 9 F, 10 F.

Continue your conversation here ...

Daughter

What do you like about your body? _____
_____
_____
_____

In which ways do you look like your mum? _____
_____
_____
_____
_____

Is there anything you do not like about your body? _____
_____
_____
_____

How do you feel about the ways your body is changing and developing?
_____
_____
_____
_____

What do you like to do to keep your body healthy? (Think about the food
you like, exercise you enjoy and how you relax.) _____
_____
_____
_____
_____

33

Mother

What do you like about your body? _____
_____
_____
_____

How does your daughter resemble you? _____
_____
_____
_____
_____

How old were you when you started your periods? What do you
remember feeling about developing and growing? _____
_____
_____
_____
_____
_____

What do you like to do to keep your body healthy? _____
_____
_____
_____
_____

Describe what is beautiful about your daughter. _____
_____
_____
_____
_____

Joint Healthy   Living Activity

Write down a healthy recipe to cook and eat together.

Ingredients

_____
_____
_____
_____
_____

Instructions

_____
_____
_____
_____
_____
_____

Brainstorm some exercise sessions you could do together and plan times to get moving and grooving.

Continue your conversation here ...

Rest and Relaxation...

Did you know that teenagers need to sleep between 9 and 9 ½ hours each night to be alert, happy and able to study and be creative? Check if you are following these simple steps to get a great night´s sleep.

1. Have a regular bedtime.
2. Don´t watch television, use the internet or play computer games in bed.
3. Avoid caffeine, smoking, alcohol and drugs.
4. Catching up on sleep at the weekend can help, but don't lie in so long that you cannot then get up on Monday morning!

Doddle some relaxation ideas here...

Continue your  conversation here ...

"Your beauty should not come from outward adornment, such as braided hair and the wearing of gold jewellery and fine clothes. Instead it should be that of your inner self, the unfading beauty of a gentle and quiet spirit, which is of great worth in God's sight." 1 Peter 3: 3-4

Daughter

These verses do not mean we should not do our hair and wear smart clothes. They are saying these are not what make us beautiful. What is true beauty? _____

_____

_____

_____

The Holy Spirit living in us produces fruit in us that is truly beautiful.

"The fruit of the Spirit is love, joy, peace, patience, kindness, goodness, faithfulness, gentleness and self-control." Galatians 5: 22.

Can you think of someone you know who is loving, gentle and kind?
What do you like most about them?
Draw and write about them below...

Mother

Can you think of someone who displays many of these fruits of the Spirit? Describe that person, and how they have been kind to you. Do you think of them as a beautiful person?

_____

_____

_____

_____

_____

How do you try to be a more loving, kind and patient person? Doddle your ideas in the space below...

Daughter

Draw some fruit. Write the qualities you already have on the fruit in yellow. Write the qualities you want to have more of in red. (Remember the qualities are love, joy, peace, patience, kindness, goodness, faithfulness, gentleness and self-control.)

Now draw some more fruit and do the same for your mum. Which qualities does she have and which does she need to work on?

Mother

Draw some fruit. Write the qualities you already have on the fruit in yellow. Write the qualities you want to have more of in red. (Remember the qualities are love, joy, peace, patience, kindness, goodness, faithfulness, gentleness and self-control.)

Now draw some more fruit and do the same for your daughter. Which qualities does she have and which does she need to work on?

Compare your drawings. Do you agree?

Continue your conversation here ...

Mother and Daughter

Doodle some messages from God to you both on these blank pages. What does He say about you? How is He challenging you to grow? What words of affirmation, encouragement and love does He have for you?

Our Family

Mother

Tell me (your daughter) about a good memory from your childhood.

_____
_____
_____

Tell me about a sad memory you have. _____

_____
_____
_____

Tell me about a time you were naughty when you were little.

_____
_____
_____
_____

Tell me how you met my Dad. Was it love at first sight?

_____
_____
_____
_____

How did you become a Christian _____

_____
_____
_____
_____

How have you kept going in the tough times? _____

_____
_____
_____

Daughter

What are the things that you always do as a family that you enjoy?

_____

_____

_____

When does your family embarrass you?

_____

_____

_____

What makes you proud of your family? _____

_____

_____

_____

_____

What do you enjoy doing with your grandparents?

_____

_____

_____

_____

Why has God put us in families?

_____

_____

_____

_____

Continue your conversation here ...

Mother

Tell me about your parents and their life like when they were young.

_____

_____
_____
_____
_____

How did they meet? _____
_____
_____
_____

Have they had any tough experiences? _____
_____
_____
_____

How would you describe my granny´s character? What kind of woman is she? _____
_____
_____
_____

How has her faith influenced her life? _____
_____
_____
_____
_____
_____

Daughter

What do you think life was like for your grandparents when they were young and did not have computer games, tablets or the internet? How did they entertain themselves and find things out?

_____

_____

_____

What do you think life was like for your great-grandparents who perhaps did not have washing machines or televisions when they married? Would you have liked living then?

_____

_____

_____

What do you think you can learn from your grandparents?

_____

_____

_____

Think of some questions you would like to ask your grandparents.

_____

_____

_____

_____

_____

_____

_____

Continue your conversation here ...

Mother

What were your family traditions when you were a girl?

_____
_____
_____
_____

What are your favourite family traditions now?

_____
_____
_____
_____

Why do you think it is important to have family traditions?

_____
_____
_____
_____

Are there any new family traditions you would like to start?

_____
_____
_____
_____
_____
_____
_____
_____
_____
_____

Daughter

What are your favourite family traditions?

_____

_____   _____

_____

Which family traditions do you like and which do you dislike?

_____

_____

_____

Would you like to change any of your family traditions?

_____

_____

_____

_____

Do you have any ideas for new family traditions?
Doodle them in the space below...

56

Daughter: These teenagers are running away from home. Give them some advice on how they could solve their problems in a different way.

"I was being bullied at school. I didn't know what to do. Mum and Dad wouldn't let me stay off school. So I ran away."

"My Mum and Dad kept arguing all the time. They were always shouting and upset. I couldn't stand it anymore so I ran away."

"I felt so lonely. No one seemed to love me, or care about me. Mum was always telling me off about something, my brother was busy with his mates and Dad was always at work. So, I ran away. If I wasn't there they wouldn't hate me anymore."

How do you think your mum would feel if you ran away?

Mother

Imagine your daughter ran away from home. How would you feel? What would you do? _____

_____

_____

_____

_____

These girls tell you why they ran away from their families. Write them some advice about different ways they could solve their problems.

"I was being bullied at school. I didn´t know what to do. Mum and Dad wouldn´t let me stay off school. So I ran away."

"My Mum and Dad kept arguing all the time. They were always shouting and upset. I couldn´t stand it anymore so I ran away."

"I felt so lonely. No one seemed to love me, or care about me. Mum was always telling me off about something, my brother was busy with his mates and Dad was always at work. So, I ran away. If I wasn´t there they wouldn´t hate me anymore."

Continue your conversation here ...

Mother & Daughter

Imagine God wrote a letter to your family. What would He say? What does He think of you? What praise does He have for you? What does He want you to do? Write your letter together here...

Living an
inspired life

Daughter

☺ Make a list of 20 things you are **thankful** for ☺

1.

2.

3.

4.

5.

6.

7.

8.

9.

10.

11.

12.

13.

14.

15.

16.

17.

18.

19.

20.

Mother

☺ Make a list of 20 things you are **thankful** for ☺

1.

2.

3.

4.

5.

6.

7.

8.

9.

10.

11.

12.

13.

14.

15.

16.

17.

18.

19.

20.

Write what is on your heart ...

Daughter

Draw a bucket and fill it with all the things you would like to do before you die.

Mother

Draw a bucket and fill it with all the things you would like to do before you die.

Mother

Write a letter to someone who has been an inspiration to you. Tell them how they were an inspiration, what they inspired you to do and how you would like to be more like them.

Dear _____,

_____

_____

_____

_____

_____

_____

_____

_____

_____

_____

_____

_____

_____

_____

_____

_____

_____

_____

_____

Love from

Daughter

Write a letter to someone who has been an inspiration to you. Tell them how they were an inspiration, what they inspired you to do and how you would like to be more like them.

Dear _____,

_____

_____

_____

_____

_____

_____

_____

_____

_____

_____

_____

_____

_____

_____

_____

_____

Love from

Write what is on your heart ...

Inspirational Women in the Bible

Read the story of Deborah together. You can find it in Judges 4. List the ways in which she was a good leader. Look at verses 4-10 particularly.

_____
_____
_____
_____
_____

Mother: Which skills did Deborah need to be a fair judge for the people?

_____
_____
_____

Daughter: Why was Deborah brave enough to go into battle?

_____
_____
_____

Mother: Why is it sometimes hard to hear and obey God?

_____
_____
_____

Daughter: Why is it sometimes hard to hear and obey God?

_____
_____
_____

Why not read the stories of Ruth, Esther and Mary (the mother of Jesus) for more inspiration?

Mother & Daughter

Imagine God gives you a vision of all He is calling you to be, the life He is calling you to live. Can you draw the vision together here?

Healthy Minds

For each of the following means of communication write down the **good**, the **bad** and the **UGLY**; what is useful about it; what is annoying about it; and when it is harmful.

Mother

	Good	Bad	UGLY
Smart Phone			
Television			
Internet			
Facebook			
Magazines			

Daughter

	Good	Bad	UGLY
Smart Phone			
Television			
Internet			
Facebook			
Magazines			

Write what is on your mind ...

Mother

Philippians 4:8 says, "Whatever is true, whatever is noble, whatever is right, whatever is pure, whatever is lovely, whatever is admirable – if anything is excellent or praiseworthy – think about such things."

Make a list of good things to think about.

_____

_____

_____

Why is it bad to fill our minds with gossip, untruths, violence, harsh words and unrealistic images? How do they make you feel?

_____

_____

_____

How can we protect our minds from dark thoughts, from thinking badly about others and ourselves?

_____

_____

_____

_____

How can we fill our minds with good, healthy thoughts? (Doodle your answer below)

Daughter

Philippians 4:8 says, "Whatever is true, whatever is noble, whatever is right, whatever is pure, whatever is lovely, whatever is admirable – if anything is excellent or praiseworthy – think about such things."

Make a list of good things to think about.

_____

_____

_____

Why is it bad to fill our minds with gossip, untruths, violence, harsh words and unrealistic images? How do they make you feel?

_____

_____

_____

How can we protect our minds from dark thoughts, from thinking badly about others and ourselves?

_____

_____

_____

_____

How can we fill our minds with good, healthy thoughts? (doodle your answer below)

Stress Quiz

Put these common sources of stress in order – 1st is the most stressful for you and 10th is the least.

1. I struggle to make ends meet financially.
2. I don't have enough hours in the day to do all that needs to be done.
3. I find it difficult to make time for all the people I love in my life.
4. I worry about what my children are doing and if they are safe.
5. I never have time alone to look after myself.
6. I worry I am not a good mother.
7. My work is stressful.
8. My health causes me stress.
9. Social media stresses me out.
10. Other people's demands on me are stressful.

Your Order:

Add some of your own sources of stress here:

Daughter

Stress Quiz

Put the following common sources of stress in order. First is the most stressful thing in your life, and 10ᵗʰ the least stressful.

1. Schoolwork, homework and the pressure to get good grades stresses me out.
2. I am stressed because my parents expect me to do well.
3. I am worried I am going to fail.
4. Problems with friends stresses me out.
5. Bullying makes me stressed.
6. My boyfriend/wanting a boyfriend makes me stressed.
7. My life is too busy.
8. Social media stresses me out.
9. I feel tired all the time and don´t get enough sleep.
10. I don´t have enough time to do the things I love to do.

Your order:

You can add other things that make you feel stressed out here:

Write what is on your mind ...

Mother

Use this page to doddle some good advice to your daughter on how to relax when she is feeling stressed. Think about ways to prioritise, learning to say "No", exercise, hobbies she enjoys, sleep, healthy food, talking things over, switching off her tablet...

Rest

Relax

Daughter

Use this page to doodle some good advice to your mother on how to relax when she is feeling stressed. Think about doing the most important thing first, learning to say "No", exercise, hobbies she enjoys, sleep, healthy food, talking things over, turning off her ´phone...

Rest

Relax

86

Mother

Do you/have you ever smoked? Why/Why not?

_____

_____

Have you ever seen anyone harmed by illegal drugs? Tell me about it.

_____

_____

_____

Do you drink alcohol? Why/Why not?

_____

_____

_____

What is your advice to me (your daughter) regarding alcohol?

_____

_____

_____

_____

What should I do if someone is pressurising me to drink/smoke/use drugs when I do not want to?

_____

_____

_____

_____

_____

_____

Daughter

Do you/have you ever smoked? Why/why not?

_____

_____

_____

What do you think the dangers of drugs are?

_____

_____

_____

What do you friends say about drugs?

_____

_____

_____

Have you drunk alcohol? Do you want to? Do you like it?

_____

_____

_____

Have you seen anyone drunk? What are the dangers of being drunk?

_____

_____

_____

Why do you think people like to get drunk?

_____

_____

_____

_____

_____

Write what is on your mind ...

Daughter

Have you ever thought about hurting yourself? Why/why not?

_____

_____

_____

Have you come across anyone at school who cuts themselves or does not eat properly (has anorexia)?

_____

_____

_____

Self-harm has become a common problem among young people. They hurt themselves physically because it is easier to deal with than an emotional pain they have. For example, Rosie felt badly about herself because she couldn't achieve the grades she wanted at school, and on Facebook, other girls were always making horrible comments about her. So, she started cutting herself to try to stop feeling so bad about herself. If Rosie was your friend and she showed you her arms with cuts on them, what would you do?

_____

_____

_____

_____

_____

If you are feeling sad and down, what things can you do to make yourself feel better? Make a big list!

Mother

If I (your daughter) am feeling pressurised, or sad or lonely or worthless, what should I do?

_____

_____

_____

_____

Have you ever felt you are not very good at anything and that other people are more beautiful, talented and clever than you? How did you cope with that?

_____

_____

_____

If you are feeling sad or angry, what do you do to express yourself?

_____

_____

_____

_____

Do you ever feel lonely or down? What do you do to make yourself feel better?

_____

_____

_____

_____

When you are an old granny and look back on your life, what will you consider a successful life?

_____

_____

_____

_____

Mother-Daughter Activity
Share the Love!

We all need to know that we are loved. Think of someone in your family who needs to hear that right now and do something creative to tell them. You could grab some warm, cheery, snug wool and knit a scarf together to give to them. Make a label telling them to wrap themself in the scarf whenever they feel sad or lonely so that they can remember they have a family that loves them.

Or find a cuddly old jumper and cut and stitch it into a cushion. Make a label telling them they can give you a hug whenever they need one.

Alternatively, make a bead necklace or bracelet together. Choose beads and charms that will suit the recipient's character and give it to them to wear as a reminder they are loved.

Alternatively, perhaps your talent is baking. Bake their favourite cake and decorate it with hearts.

On the other hand, perhaps what the person really needs is a helping hand. Go together one Saturday afternoon to mow their lawn, weed their garden, plant some bulbs or paint the fence. Alternatively, do their shopping, wash their dishes or cook them a meal.

Or perhaps they really need a listening ear.

You can come up with your own ideas... just make sure you then go and put them into action!

Write how you are feeling ...

Mother & Daughter

God wants to fill our minds with good thoughts. Fill the page with the true, wholesome, excellent words God speaks.

Emotions

Daughter

Think about a time in your life when you felt sad. What happened? How did you feel? What could you hear, see and smell? What thoughts filled your mind? What made you feel better?

Write a poem to express your sadness.

Mother

Think about a time in your life when you felt sad. What happened? How did you feel? What could you hear, see and smell? What thoughts filled your mind? What made you feel better?

Write a poem to express your sadness.

Read the story of the death of Lazarus together in John 11v1-44.

Verse 35 tell us, Jesus wept. Why was he sad?

_____

— _____

_____

Verse 19 tells us many Jews had gone to comfort Mary and Martha. How can we comfort someone when they are sad?

_____

_____

_____

_____

Read verses 25 & 26, 43 & 44 again. Jesus went to be with the sisters, to comfort them through his presence with them in their time of trouble. He also gave them hope. When bad things happen to us, what hope does Jesus offer us? What promises has he made us?

_____

_____

_____

_____

Daughter: Think of a time when you were sad. Who helped you? How?

_____

_____

_____

_____

Mother: Think of a time you were sad. Who helped you? How?

_____

_____

_____

_____

Write how you are feeling ...

Daughter

What **scares** you? List your fears here.

_____
_____
_____
_____

Sometimes fear is a **warning** to us to be careful. For example, we are
scared to jump from a height because if we do we might hurt ourselves.
Are any of your fears ones that warn you to be careful? Which ones?

_____
_____
_____
_____
_____

Sometimes, we need to **face our fears**. For example, God might ask us
to talk to a friend about Jesus, but we are scared to do it. In this case, we
should be courageous and do the thing that we are afraid of. Are any of
your fears in this category? Which ones?

_____
_____
_____
_____
_____

Mother

What **scares** you? List your fears here.

_____

_____

_____

_____

Sometimes fear is a **warning** to us to be careful. For example, we are scared to jump from a height because if we do we might hurt ourselves. Are any of your fears ones that warn you to be careful? Which ones?

_____

_____

_____

_____

Sometimes we need to **face our fears**. For example, God might ask us to talk to a friend about Jesus, but we are scared to do it. In this case, we should be courageous and do the thing that we are afraid of. Are any of your fears in this category? Which ones?

_____

_____

_____

_____

_____

_____

_____

Be Brave!

Memorization Challenge

Can you memorize two passages that are helpful to bring to mind whenever you feel afraid?

"Have I not commanded you? **Be strong and courageous.** Do not be terrified; do not be discouraged, for **the Lord your God will be with you** wherever you go." Joshua 1 v 9

"I lift up my eyes to the hills –
Where does my help come from?
**My help comes from the Lord,
The maker of heaven and earth.**
He will not let your foot slip.
He who watches over you will not slumber;
Indeed, he who watches over Israel will neither slumber nor sleep.
The Lord watches over you –
The Lord is your shade at your right hand;
The sun will not harm you by day,
Nor the moon by night.
The Lord will keep you from all harm-
He will watch over your life;
The Lord will watch over your coming and your going
Both **now and for evermore.**" Psalm 121

Write how you are feeling ...

Daughter

When are you happy?

_____

_____

_____

_____

Celebrations are an important part of life, which help to counteract the sad times. Draw your ideal birthday celebration here:

Mother

When are you happy?

_____ _____
_____
_____
_____

Celebrations are an important part of life, which help to counteract the
sad times. What do you like to celebrate? Draw your ideal celebration
here:

Write what you are feeling...

Daughter

What makes you angry? Write your answers here in **bold** letters.

Are you right to be angry about these things?

_____
_____
_____
_____

What do you do when you are angry?

_____
_____
_____
_____

Ephesians 4 v 26 says, **"In your anger do not sin."** What do you think that means?

_____
_____
_____
_____
_____
_____

Mother

What makes you angry? Write your answers here in **bold** letters.

Are you right to be angry about these things?

_____
_____
_____
_____

What do you do when you are angry?

_____
_____
_____
_____

Ephesians 4 v 26 says, **"In your anger do not sin."** What do you think that means?

_____
_____
_____
_____
_____
_____

Read Matthew 21 v 12-16 together.

Why was Jesus angry?

_____

_____

_____

Was he right to be angry?

_____

_____

_____

Why were the **chief priests** angry? (Verse 15)

_____

_____

_____

Were they right to be?

_____

_____

_____

Daughter: Think of something you are **right** to be **angry** about. What are you going to do about it?

_____

_____

_____

Mother: Think of something you are **not** right to be **angry** about. What do you need to do to calm down?

_____

_____

_____

Write what you are feeling ...

Mother & Daughter

How does God feel about you? Write the emotions He feels creatively on this page together.

Growing Up

Mother

When Jesus was 12 years old, he was taken to the temple to celebrate embarking on manhood. What rites of passage have you had in your life? Did you celebrate your teeth falling out? Did you mark starting to menstruate in any way? Did you have any special birthdays? Tell me about these events.

_____

_____

_____

_____

_____

Have you had any special events that have marked your faith journey? Have you been baptised, confirmed or become a member of a church? Tell me about them.

_____

_____

_____

_____

_____

Which special days would you like to celebrate in my (your daughter's) life?

_____

_____

_____

_____

_____

Daughter

When Jesus was 12 years old, he was taken to the temple to celebrate embarking on manhood. You are growing and changing all the time. Which events in your life have you enjoyed celebrating? (Teeth falling out, becoming a teenager, baptism, menstruation, a special birthday, a special achievement at school....)

_____

_____

_____

_____

What would you like to celebrate as you grow up? List the events here and any ideas you have about how you would like to celebrate. Do you want a party? A family meal? An outing with your aunties? A trip somewhere special? A particular gift?

Daughter

Use this page to write a letter to your **18-year-old self**. Think about what you think you will be doing and enjoying at this age. Do you have questions for her? Do you have advice to give her? Do you want to tell her about things you hope she is doing and experiencing? Let your imagination run riot.

Dear 18-year-old self,

_____

_____

_____

_____

_____

_____

_____

_____

_____

_____

_____

_____

_____

_____

_____

_____

_____

_____

_____

_____

_____

Lots of love from

Mother

Look back at yourself as an **18 year old**. What were you like then?
What were you doing? What were your hopes for the future? Write a
letter to your 18-year-old self, telling her about what has happened since
that time, expressing how you feel about it.

Dear 18-year-old self,

_____

_____

_____

_____

_____

_____

_____

_____

_____

_____

_____

_____

_____

_____

_____

_____

_____

_____

_____

_____

_____

_____

_____

Lots of love from

Any questions? ...

Daughter

Describe what you hope to do this summer.

_____

_____

_____

_____

_____

Draw what you would like to be doing in 3 years' time.

Imagine yourself in 10 years´ time. What are you like? What are you doing? Who are you with?

Mother

Describe what you hope to do this summer.

_____

_____

_____

_____

_____

Draw what you would like to be doing in 3 years' time.

Imagine yourself in 10 years´ time. What are you like? What are you doing? Who are you with?

Daughter

Read Matthew 6 v 19-21

"Do not store up for yourself treasures on earth, where moth and rust destroy and where thieves break in and steal. But store up for yourselves treasures in heaven, where moth and rust do not destroy, and where thieves do not break in and steal. For where your treasure is, there your heart will be also."

Are your **ambitions** generous towards other people? Will they help build up your family and community? Alternatively, are they selfish, mainly for your own benefit?

Write down your ambitions on this page. Colour those that will help others in some way, green. Colour those that are just about you, red.

Mother

Read Matthew 6 v 19-21

"Do not store up for yourself treasures on earth, where moth and rust destroy and where thieves break in and steal. But store up for yourselves treasures in heaven, where moth and rust do not destroy, and where thieves do not break in and steal. For where your treasure is, there your heart will be also."

Are your **ambitions** generous towards other people? Will they help build up your family and community? Alternatively, are they selfish, mainly for your own benefit?

Write down your ambitions on this page. Colour those that will help others in some way, green. Colour those that are just about you, red.

Any questions? ...

Daughter

Write a list of 20 **random acts of kindness** you could do for others.

1

2

3

4

5

6

7

8

9

10

11

12

13

14

15

16

17

18

19

20

Now look at your mum´s list. Who has been the most creative? Who will actually do some of them?

Mother

Write a list of 20 **random acts of kindness** you could do for others.

1

2

3

4

5

6

7

8

9

10

11

12

13

14

15

16

17

18

19

20

Write what you are feeling ...

Taking
Responsibility
For Your Life

Daughter

An important part of being a teenager is learning to **take responsibility** for your own life. Take this quick quiz to find out how you are doing. If you do **the chore** listed **all the time**, put a tick in that column. If you have only done it **occasionally**, put a tick in the **"Have done it once"** column. If you have **never** done it, then put a tick in the **"not a clue"** column.

Chore	Not a clue	Have done it once	I do it all the time
Wash the dishes			
Clean & tidy my room			
Hoover & dust			
Clean the bathroom			
Cook meals for the family			
Mend and fix things e.g. clothes & appliances			
Save up my money to buy something big.			
Take responsibility for caring for a pet.			
Look after younger siblings or cousins.			
Organise a party or special event.			
I can earn or raise money for a charity or myself.			
Sort and put out rubbish/recycling.			

Now **add up your score.**

Give yourself **2 points** for every tick in the **"Do it all the time"** column.

Give yourself **1 point** for every tick in the **"done it once"** column.

You don't get any points if you have never done it!

MY GRAND TOTAL:

If you scored 0-8 points: Now is the time to start learning these vital life skills. You will need them in order to live a successful, independent life, so pick the one you want to learn first and have a go!

If you scored 9-16 points: Well done, you are taking responsibility for your life and have already learnt some important life skills. Now pick the next one you want to learn and have a go. Keep learning!

If you scored 18-24 points: You are an accomplished young person. Excellent. Keep putting these life skills into practice to make your home and community a better place.

Mother

Put these domestic chores in order. Put the one you **like doing most, first** and your **pet hate, last**...

Washing dishes

Vacuuming

Dusting

Cleaning the bathroom

Putting out the rubbish

Walking the dog

Mowing the lawn

Cleaning the car

Cooking meals

Shopping

Tidying up

Changing the sheets on the beds

Ironing

Mending

Gardening/watering plants

<u>Which chores would you most appreciate help with?</u>

-
-
-
-
-

133

Write what comes to mind...

Daughter

Why will you need to have a job when you are an adult?

_____

_____

_____

Describe your dream job.

_____

_____

_____

What will you need to do in order to get that job?

_____

_____

_____

_____

What will you do if you don´t get a job you really want?

_____

_____

_____

_____

What will you do if you find your job boring?

_____

_____

_____

_____

_____

_____

Mother

What paid jobs have you had in your lifetime?

_____

_____

_____

Which ones have you enjoyed? Why?

_____

_____

_____

Which ones did you not enjoy? Why?

_____

_____

_____

What have you done when you have found jobs boring? How have you kept going?

_____

_____

_____

_____

What do you think are important things to consider when choosing a career?

_____

_____

_____

_____

_____

_____

_____

Mother-Daughter Activity

Choose a job you can do together. It could be something that needs doing around your **own home** or garden, or you could volunteer to **help someone else**. Perhaps a job needs doing in your **church or community**.

Once you have done the job together, take time to reflect on the experience on this page. Each write in a different coloured pen, so you can see whose thoughts are whose.

Answer these questions:
- What you enjoyed & did not enjoy.
- Whom you helped.
- How you contributed to your family or community.
- Why it is important to work to help others.
- How you feel about the experience.

Mother – Colour in all the countries you have visited in **yellow**, and those you would like to visit in **red**. **Daughter** colour in the countries you have visited in **pink** and those you would like to visit in **purple**.

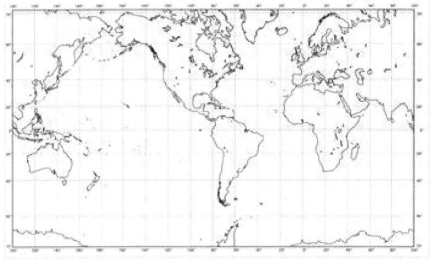

Mother: Where is your favourite place in the world and why?

Daughter: Where is your favourite place in the world and why?

Mother: Where would you most like to visit and why?

Daughter: Where would you most like to visit and why?

Mother & Daughter

Sometimes taking responsibility for our decisions and ourselves can be scary. What promises does God give us as we step out in faith and obedience? Write them together on this page

Friends

Mother

Who was your first friend? Are you still in touch?

_____

_____

Have your friends changed over the years? Who are your best friends
now?_____

_____

_____

Tell me about a good friend of yours.

_____

_____

_____

_____

Tell me about a bad friend.

_____

_____

_____

Tell me about a time a friend hurt you.

_____

_____

_____

_____

Tell me about a time a friend brought you joy.

_____

_____

_____

_____

Daughter

Who was your first friend? What do you remember about them?

_____

_____

_____

Who are your friends now? Why did you choose them to be your friends?

_____

_____

_____

_____

Tell me about a time a friend hurt you.

_____

_____

_____

_____

Tell me about a time a friend helped you.

_____

_____

_____

_____

_____

What do you most like to chat about with your friends?

_____

_____

_____

_____

Write what comes to mind...

Dilemmas

You meet up with some other mums for a coffee and a chat. Someone starts gossiping about a friend of yours, who is not present. You do not like what they are saying about her and know that half of it is not true anyway. What do you do?

_____

_____

_____

_____

Some work colleagues are talking about religion and are saying some hateful things about Christians. You are listening to their conversation. How do you feel? What do you do?

_____

_____

_____

_____

A friend of yours comes to see you for a chat. She tells you her boss at work is sexually harassing her. She really needs the work and does not know what to do. What would you advise her?

_____

_____

_____

_____

A Christian friend of yours is talking about doing something that you consider foolish and wrong. She tells you about it and asks your opinion. How would you respond? Would you give your honest opinion or would you be afraid of hurting her feelings?

_____

_____

Daughter

Dilemmas

A group of schoolmates are gossiping about a friend of yours. You are in the group and know your friend would be most upset if she knew what they were saying about her. What do you do?

_____

_____

_____

_____

A group of your friends invite you to go with them to do something that your mum has told you not to do. Would you go? Why or why not?

_____

_____

_____

_____

Your friend asks you to cover for her while she goes out with her boyfriend. Her mum has forbidden her to go on this occasion. What would you do?

_____

_____

_____

_____

A friend asks your opinion on her new outfit. You think it looks awful. What do you say?

_____

_____

_____

_____

Mother

List 20 things you **love to do with your friends.**

1

2

3

4

5

6

7

8

9

10

11

12

13

14

15

16

17

18

19

20

147

Daughter

List 20 things you **love to do with your friends**

1

2

3

4

5

6

7

8

9

10

11

12

13

14

15

16

17

18

19

20

Write what comes to mind...

Mother

Tell me about your first boyfriend. What was he like? How long were you an item? How did it end?

_____

_____

_____

_____

Tell me about your first kiss.

_____

_____

_____

_____

Do you have any regrets about boys you went out with or things you did with them? Did anyone pressure you into doing things that you did not want to?

_____

_____

_____

_____

What was the best advice you were given about dating?

_____

_____

_____

What did you enjoy most about having a boyfriend?

_____

_____

_____

Daughter

Do you think you are attractive to boys? Why or why not?

_____

_____

_____

_____

Do you want to have a boyfriend? Why or why not?

_____

_____

_____

_____

Has a boyfriend ever put pressure on you to do things you do not want to? Write about it here.

_____

_____

_____

_____

Make a list of fun things to do on dates.

_____

_____

_____

_____

When you have a boyfriend, how does it affect your other friendships?

_____

_____

_____

_____

How far is too far?

Fill in the table to show if you think the following actions are acceptable while you are dating someone. If you think they are, then mark "yes". If you think that you should wait until you are married, then mark "no".

Mother

	YES	NO
Kissing		
Cuddles		
Necking/love bites		
Touching above the waist		
Touching below the waist		
Sexual intercourse		

Daughter

	YES	NO
Kissing		
Cuddles		
Necking/love bites		
Touching above the waist		
Touching below the waist		
Sexual intercourse		

Mother

♡ Does **true** *love* **wait**? Why or why not? ♡

Daughter

♡ Does **true** *love* **wait**? Why or why not? ♡

Keep the conversation flowing...

Daughter

Draw and annotate a picture of your ideal man.
What does he look like?
What kind of person is he?
What does he like to do?
Is he a Christian?
How old do you think you will be when you marry?

Mother

Use this space to write a prayer for your daughter's future husband. What do you desire for her?

Dear Heavenly Father,

Amen

Mother

Has anyone ever bullied you? What happened? How did you feel?

_____
_____
_____
_____
_____
_____

How did you cope with it?

_____
_____
_____
_____
_____

What advice would you give to someone who is being bullied?

_____
_____
_____
_____
_____
_____

Daughter

Has anyone ever bullied you? What happened and how did you feel?

_____

_____

_____

_____

_____

_____

How did you cope with it?

_____

_____

_____

_____

_____

_____

What would you do if a friend of yours is being bullied?

_____

_____

_____

_____

_____

_____

What can you do about online bullying?

_____

_____

_____

_____

_____

_____

Mother

Bullying damages your self-esteem.

Use this space to write down your **strengths**, the things you do best, **what is great about you** and the **best experiences** you have had.

Around the edge note down the names of the **people who love you** best.

Daughter

Bullying damages your self-esteem.

Use this space to write down your **strengths**, the things you do best, **what is great about you** and the **best experiences** you have had.

Around the edge note down the names of the **people who love you** best.

Keep the conversation flowing...

_____
_____
_____
_____
_____
_____
_____
_____
_____
_____
_____
_____
_____
_____
_____
_____
_____
_____
_____
_____
_____
_____
_____
_____
_____
_____
_____

Mother

How do you feel when you need to say sorry?

_____
_____
_____
_____
_____

How do you feel when someone else apologises to you?

_____
_____
_____
_____
_____

Tell me about a time when it was hard to forgive.

_____
_____
_____
_____
_____

How do you feel when you refuse to forgive?

_____
_____
_____
_____
_____

Daughter

How do you feel when you need to say sorry?

_____

_____

_____

_____

_____

How do you feel when someone else apologises to you?

_____

_____

_____

_____

_____

Tell me about a time when it was hard to forgive.

_____

_____

_____

_____

_____

How do you feel when you refuse to forgive?

_____

_____

_____

_____

_____

Mother & Daughter

Forgiveness is at the heart of our relationship with God. Imagine God writes you a message of love and forgiveness. What does it say? Write it together here.

_____

_____

_____

_____

_____

_____

_____

_____

_____

_____

_____

_____

_____

_____

_____

_____

_____

_____

_____

_____

_____

_____

_____

Community

Mother

Tell me a favourite memory from your school days.

_____
_____
_____
_____
_____

Tell me a worst memory from your school days.

_____
_____
_____
_____
_____

Tell me about your favourite teacher. Who was he/she and what were they like? Why did you like them?

_____
_____
_____
_____
_____

What were your best and worst subjects at school?

_____
_____
_____

Which sports did you play?

_____
_____
_____
_____

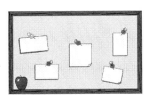

Daughter

Who is your favourite teacher? Why?

_____
_____
_____
_____
_____

Who are your friends at school/clubs you attend? What is great about them?

_____
_____
_____
_____
_____

What is fun about school/studying?

_____
_____
_____
_____
_____

What problems do you have at school/ in your studies?

_____
_____
_____
_____
_____

Keep the conversation flowing...

Keep the conversation flowing...

Mother

Draw a picture of your **church**. On your picture write or draw the things you like and dislike about church. Show how church is a family for you. Show the things that help your faith to grow. Show the opportunities you have to serve.

Daughter

Draw a picture of your **church**. On your picture write or draw the things you like and dislike about church. Show how church is a family for you. Show the things that help your faith to grow. Show the opportunities you have to serve.

Keep the conversation flowing...

Mother

Write a letter to your daughter telling her what you have learnt about her by doing this journal with her.

Dear

_____

_____

_____

_____

_____

_____

_____

_____

_____

_____

_____

_____

_____

_____

_____

_____

_____

_____

_____

_____

_____

_____

_____

_____

Love from

Daughter

Write a letter to your mother telling her what you have learnt about her by doing this journal with her.

Dear Mum,

_____
_____
_____
_____
_____
_____
_____
_____
_____
_____
_____
_____
_____
_____
_____
_____
_____
_____
_____
_____
_____
_____
_____
_____
_____
_____
_____

Love from

Keep the conversation flowing...

Daughter

Write a prayer for your mother.

Mother

Write a prayer for your daughter.

This does not have to be the end of your journaling experience together. If you have enjoyed writing to each other, then why not grab a blank journal and keep going. Keep on writing your thoughts, questions, feelings, hopes and fears. Keep on deepening your precious and wonderful relationship.

About the Author

Andrea Gardiner is a mother of three daughters. She grew up attending the Girls' Brigade in England, and served as an officer and on the National Training Committee of Girls' Brigade Scotland until she moved to Ecuador in 2005. She worked as a medical missionary for 13 years. She now works as a GP in Scotland and continues to run the charity Project Ecuador, running health prevention programmes, girls' clubs and camps, and a child sponsorship scheme.

You can find out more about her work on
www.projectecuador.co.uk

Andrea Gardiner is also the author of

30 Days of Prayer for your Daughter
&
30 Days of prayer for your Son
Interactive Prayer Journals

Guinea Pig for Breakfast and **Guinea Pig for Brunch** –
Biographies of her life as a missionary doctor in Ecuador

Jeff Lucas comments,
"The inspiring accounts of a true adventurer."

And

The **Tamarita Rachel** series
Stories for 4-8 year olds about the everyday adventures of
children living in Ecuador. They teach Christian values and the
challenges of missionary life in an engaging and fun way.

Coming soon...

Free-Fall: A Journal for the Autumn Season of Life.
A journal full of spiritual practices to guide you through
a time of loss or transition.

All available on Amazon website

Printed in Great Britain
by Amazon